The unimaginable story that takes you through the emotions of hurt, grief, anger, and sadness to eventually find happiness through hope and healing.

I0528408

GIVING
into hope

KRISTA J. SOBIESKI

ISBN: 978-1-960136-92-3

Table of Contents

Original words by Krista Sobieski

Healing Through the Unimaginable
The Hurt That Heals
The Empty Chair
The Nightmare Before
The Light that Comes
Life, Love, and Relationships
No Obstacles in the Way

Introduction

The greatest spiritual battle we have, sometimes is in our own mind. We face challenges and without proper coping mechanisms and support, we face the grim reality that we will all go through hurt, grief, anger, and sadness. Hope at times may be the one emotion that can help us hold on and lead us to the stage of happiness and joy that we deserve.

In *Giving into Hope*, Krista J. Sobieski takes you through a reflection of her life. It is a story of success, failure, trials, tribulations, and heartache. Bad things *do* happen to good people, and the hope is that this story will help you to accept what is, regain control, and move forward as your authentic self so that you can heal, love, and find happiness in life again. It is a story of strength and one of will and determination that proves when you hold onto hope, you can push through and make choices that will bring you back to a positive place and understand that there is power in stepping up and overcoming loss, betrayal, and heartache.

This book will help you find a way to move forward, help get through the hard times to eventually find the light that comes after the darkness! There is always hope, always, and when you give into it, life can become better with a positive mindset.

Author Krista J. Sobieski created the Thoughtful Seed Project, a professional writing service, allowing her the opportunity to help others with their writing and training needs. Through this book, she has shared her authentic story, shared in her own words.

She is also willing to share it in person, doing speaking engagements and personal appearances. Her hope is to inspire others, by providing them the encouragement and hope they need to overcome any challenge they face. Holding on and giving into hope, sometimes is the last saving grace a person has, and like the author, everyone can push through any dilemma.

What to Expect in This Book

This book about the reality of life will take you through hurt, grief, anger, sadness, happiness, and, eventually, hope. It is the story of a journey that seems unreal, unimaginable really. It's a story that forces reflection on the life that one expected and thought they had. It is a story of success, failure, trials, tribulations, and heartache. Bad things *do* happen to good people, and my hope is that this story will help you to accept what is, regain control, and move forward as your authentic self so that you can heal, love, and find happiness in life again. It is a story of strength and will to create a life that is better than you may have imagined.

This book is not just about death, grieving, and overcoming pain, but about pushing through challenges, leading to a success mindset that will help you find a way to take the hurt that heals and use it to get over the troubles and get going! My hope is that it will help you to prioritize and learn that the small stuff in life is the big stuff, and that you have to allow yourself time to feel, heal, and navigate through the emotions of life to live happily. You will find a way to move forward, but you must get through the hard stuff to find the light that comes after the darkness! There is always hope, always, and when you give into it, life can become better with a positive mindset.

Healing Through the Unimaginable

My story is one of unimaginable hurt and unimaginable loss, and just when I thought I had been through enough, my unimaginable story changed me and my life forever. Life is hard; life is full of things that will knock us down, but what I learned is that when we show our emotions and share our stories, it helps us heal. My story is unique to me, and what I want to give by sharing it is a bright outlook that will inspire and give hope. Just like me, when you think your story is too hard to share, you realize that by doing so, you can give a gift. When you give in to hope, you can change the state of your life. I hope this story can help you by giving you the power to persevere and move on through the most difficult times in life. Feeling numb is real, and experiencing the greatest shock can zap the passion and life out of your soul. *Giving in to Hope* is a gift that I can give, and by sharing my story, I can help others to find the hope that has carried me.

We have to love ourselves, not blame ourselves for what we feel. Remember, feelings are real. We can't worry about the past, looking back at what we had or at what we can't get back. We have to allow ourselves to go through the emotions and accept that some situations we may never get over. Yet, in time, we will learn to make peace and we will learn to live again. The greatest gift we can give ourselves is to love ourselves and be our greatest selves by honoring who we truly are. We have to stop wanting and needing approval from others and stop judging ourselves; we need to start celebrating ourselves. We should be glad that our true colors are like the stripes of a zebra and match no other—it's what makes us unique. We are meant to be celebrated for all that we are, to live a life without fear and resentment, and to overcome our greatest challenges.

We have to learn that we are human and we will make choices—they might not always be the right ones, but that is what is so magical about life; without exploration and without wonder, we really never move forward, and like me, you can move forward.

Sometimes, like me, you might feel like you are moving mountains but not getting anywhere. Like me, you might feel like you are carrying the weight of burdens on your shoulders and questioning how things can get so bad when they have been so good. Just when you think things can't get worse, you realize they can and they will. Sometimes, life brings us back to reality to help us realize that really bad things can happen to really good people. What we do after turmoil and loss is what defines us. Our successes and failures are part of our lives, and how we stand up after we fall is where our legacy is created.

It is very important to be authentic. Thinking about authenticity, it is important to remember why it matters and what is important. As a person you should remain true to your values in the face of external pressures and expectations, and still be able to think and behave a certain way. When you come from an authentic place, it is less likely that you will allow external pressures to change who you really are. True happiness comes from a place where you know what you think and feel and, even though you are not perfect, you have grace enough to share from a place of compassion and authenticity.

Authenticity is not just about honesty or consistency; it transcends those qualities. When you are authentic, you are not acting; you are in alignment with your true self, your core values, and your unique personality. It can be very hard under pressure to remain authentic, yet it's vital, especially when you are in roles of leadership, in the workplace, in your home, and in your heart.

Authenticity involves being true to yourself and understanding what motivates you, moves you, and helps you find your passion. It's about knowing what you like, how your emotions flow, and your abilities. When you act congruently with this self-knowledge, you're being authentic.

While authenticity is about sharing truths, it really goes deeper than this. Sometimes, we withhold certain things without intending to hold back, yet sometimes if we cannot reveal everything, it does not always mean we are not authentic. It can mean that, for underlying reasons, there is something that may hold us back, perhaps judgment, fear, or concern that we may be misunderstood. When we can't be authentic, it creates issues, internally and externally. Not sharing my story did not allow me to be authentic and I knew that, yet it has still been holding me back.

Striving to be authentic doesn't mean you're being your true self all the time; it means aligning your actions to match what you are doing and saying as well as leading with integrity. Through this book, I hope that those reading can feel my authenticity, and that the book can share the truth of my story to make a difference in the lives of others. In toxic environments, it's hard to be authentic, and when leaders are not living authentically, it can result in fear and stress. When you help others overcome fears and express vulnerabilities, it helps to liberate you from pretense and allows you to embrace imperfections. Not all leaders encompass this trait, and it can become quite dicey when leaders do not strive for authenticity and do not allow those under them to be authentic as well.

Authenticity comes from knowing what's important to you and remaining true to those values despite being pressured or feeling like you cannot meet the requirements by being put in situations where you are forced to question your own morals and values. Toxic people create toxic environments, and anyone who does not allow for authenticity and harness how valuable it can be for productivity, families, and work relations, will never succeed as a leader.

When you navigate from an authentic place, you're truer to who you are, have strong self-awareness, and create a better environment. You will be happier and so will the others around you.

In essence, authenticity isn't about perfection; it's about embracing your genuine self, flaws and all. It can be hard, I understand. Self-love can be hard, and self-sabotage can get the best of all of us, yet it all comes back to authenticity. Authenticity is important and it's vital in how we think about ourselves and those around us, and how we go forth in the world. Be authentic, your life will be a lot better because of it; and if you can't be for underlying reasons like me, then find the courage to share your story. It can help free you.

The Hurt That Heals

A mother's unconditional love is one of the greatest gifts that can be given to us growing up. Mothers have the single greatest influence on a child. Research proves that even before birth, moms have a strong influence on our lives. Mothers play a crucial role in our lives as they nurture, support, and guide us through our journey in life. They help shape our character and provide unconditional love. The relationship we have with our mothers has a great bearing on how we interact with others and how we view ourselves.

(Photo: My mother was one of the most influential people in my life. She is irreplaceable, although all she taught me has remained with me. I am grateful I had a mom like her.)

My mom was one of the strongest women I knew. Growing up, my mom seemed like a superwoman, one who could master anything thrown at her. She was a jack of all trades, as one might say. Give her a needle and thread, and she will make you something. Give her a pan and some food and she will feed you. Give her some dirt and some seeds and she will grow your food. Give her a hammer and nail and she will build you something. Give her a wrench and a screwdriver and she will fix what is broken. My mom was one of the single most amazing people when it came to taking nothing and making something wonderful out of it. She was creative and resourceful and had a home remedy for resolving most situations.

She was not perfect, but she was strong, courageous, and one of the hardest-working people I knew. She used tough love and didn't let her guard down or skip a beat when telling you to "wipe away those tears and get over it." Her position was to get up, get over it, and get moving because there is much more to do than just stand around wiping tears away.

My mom was one of the most influential people in my life, so finding out that she was terminally ill was one of the single most defining moments in my life. My guide, my protector, my mother was going to die. *How could this be?* I thought. *I am already going through hell right now and I need her here to help me through it.* That might seem selfish, but between my mom being diagnosed with cancer in 2011 and metastatic breast cancer in 2016, I was already living a silent nightmare and my mom was supposed to help see me through it. I didn't have time for her to have cancer. There's more on my silent nightmare in another chapter, but how could this woman that I so desperately needed be planning to leave me? How was I going to manage losing her? It seemed unimaginable to me going through it then, but in time, it was my mother's very own idea that began to help me find a way to make the hurt heal.

(Photo: Christmas season, 1975. I am the baby; my mom, Marge Minsky, is holding me, along with my sisters, having our photo taken with Santa. Looking at it reminds me of a mom's role in shaping who we are.)

I was reminded of this photo that was taken during the holidays, and it resonated with me for many reasons. I was a baby, so I was too young to remember the events of the photo, but looking back, it reminds me of the simple things; simple times and the love that a mother has for her children. It also reminds me of my mom and how she raised my two sisters I to be independent and strong. We all miss her, and I miss the unconditional love she had for me, my siblings, her grandchildren, and those she loved. When I reflect on this photo, now that my mom is gone, I think so much about her, wondering about that stage of her life and what her hopes, her wishes, and her dreams were at that time. Like most mothers, I presume she wanted a bright future for us as her kids and to give us the best life she could.

I think I am drawn to this photo because for the first time, after her death, I see the reflection of myself in my mother. When

I look at this photo, it reminds me how much more alike we are than I ever thought. I never thought much about being like my mom. I just thought of her as a mom. This photo shows the goodness and the happiness that was in her, yet I know that what it does not show is the fear that she may have had as a young mother of three, the troubles she may have been going through at the time, or the stress that she had as a young married woman living on her husband's salary. It doesn't tell the story of how she gave up her own dreams to be a stay-at-home mom so she could give the best to her kids, living paycheck to paycheck and wondering what was next. It shows the joy of a mother who had nothing but pure love for the three girls that she brought into the world.

Thinking about my mother and looking beyond the smile in this photo, I reflect on myself and how I can relate very much to her. The happy moments are what keep us going and what most of us strive for in life, for ourselves and for our families. I can relate to what it is like to raise young children, having four of my own, and I know how much time and effort it takes. For the first time, looking back, I really appreciate my mom on a new level. The reflection is suddenly there. Even though we are very different, we are all very much alike.

My mom was independent, strong, and seemed to have a solution for every problem in life. She did her job, she raised her children and set us free. She gave us to the world to embrace it as we wanted and let it be. She did not interfere, meddle, or do harm, she just did her job and then let it be. Now, as I find myself missing her more with each passing moment, this photo means so much more to me. It reminds me of a woman who I thought I never wanted to be. Looking at it these days, I understand how much she is always going to be a part of me. When I am weak, it is her love that guides me; when I need courage, it is her love that helps me roar, and when I need strength, it is her love that holds me up. My impression of my mom has changed a lot over the years, and perhaps she is exactly who I hope I can be: a mother who unconditionally loves her children and one day is able to set them free with grace and dignity, and then be grateful when they come home.

My mom gave me the strength to go on, so there was no other choice but to move on. Breast cancer, any cancer is like an evil hell that strips a body's strength and wounds the soul so deeply. Mom had courage but chose to allow herself to be pain-free, and no longer wanted to endure the battle. Cancer raged in her body and after three months of intense treatment, she said no more. Mom held on long enough to give us time, because she loved her family. Moving on without her is what I had to do, but why did I have to move on unexpectedly without Dad too?

Yet somehow, it's like Mom prepared me. Mom always said, "We live to die." *We live to die* sounds so profound to me, so final, yet the truth behind it is that death can happen at any time, at any moment. My mom found a way to put the grace in living to die. Her words at the time, prior to her own death, did not seem as profound, though now they are. I wasn't really sure how to live to die, and though I don't honestly think she knew, with her words she prepared me for my dad's death. I do not think that my mom knew that my dad was having serious health issues, but

I do think that she was using her unconditional love and words to help me accept the hurdles that I may face. There was no way to prepare for the next chapter, *The Empty Chair*, without Dad, too, yet in my heart, even if I didn't believe it at the time, she prepared me. My life forever changed on February 2, 2017.

The Empty Chair

When your mom is going to die and you know it, if your dad is still living and they are together like mine had been for nearly fifty years, the last thing you think about is losing him too. You can't imagine the heartache he is feeling having lost the person he has spent the majority of his life with. It's sad to think about his chair being empty too, and most people don't even imagine that until reality strikes and you realize that you have found that your dad has died too.

When you think things can't get worse, they might. The same night my mom died, only three short hours later, I found my dad, too. He was dead in his chair.

Walking into their home, knowing my mom would never be back, was enough to bring sadness to my heart and tears to my eyes. What I didn't expect was that walking back through that door, into my parents' home, I would find my father gone too. So suddenly, he was gone. Could it be, was it real, or was I dreaming about this? Was this a real tragedy that had actually just happened? Screaming, "Dad, dad, dad," and there was no response. What was going on? Why was my dad not answering me? There was no movement, no breath. His clenched face and large body sat lifeless in the chair and I needed help. Everything was crazy, but time seemed to be moving so slowly. I needed help.

Calling 911, it was hard to understand; there was no pulse, no breath, no movement, just his warm, strong, structured body in a chair, peaceful, calm, and unbelievably free. How could this be?

It was real—my dad had died too.

Just 42 minutes earlier I was talking to him, talking about my mom and the awful anger we had that her life could not be spared. His sad voice was uncertain about how he would go on without her, yet calming to ensure that I was alright too. It didn't seem possible that the man I had just spent 25 minutes talking to on the phone was now dead too.

The police officers and emergency personnel all came to help, removing his lifeless body from the chair; his favorite red reclining chair was now empty. As I stood there in shock, in my parents' dining room watching, not sure what was happening or what to do, I witnessed them work on my father. Breaths, chest compressions, an AED machine attempting to bring my father back to life weren't working. A neighbor and my husband arrived on the scene, too. I remember my husband's screams as he walked in: "Oh my god, oh my god, how can this be happening, too? Come on, Stevie, we can't lose you too."

How could this be? Was it real? It could not be possible, that I had just watched my mother peacefully lose her battle with cancer and now my dad's chair is empty and he is dead too.

Sadness in his eyes, uncertain of just what to do, I remember an officer looking at me, trying to find the best words to officially share the news.

"I am sorry," he said. "I don't know what to say. I understand you lost your mother earlier and there is nothing we could do to save your father today. We tried but it wasn't to be, his heart must have just been broken beyond repair today. I am so sorry, I just don't know what else to say."

One officer found me a chair so I could sit down and try to breathe, while the others attempted to reassure me that everything would be okay. Deep sadness in their eyes, words of comfort as they, themselves tried to understand. One by one they hugged me, sensing my pain and watching my tears drain. There were no words as we all turned to look; all that was there was that empty red chair. Their shaky voices, their hearts broken just as much as mine, they tried so hard to do their job, but it wasn't meant to be, there just was not enough time.

Three officers standing still, with heads slightly bowed; it's then that you realize this awful moment forever becomes their memory, too. Forever an empty red chair will define that moment in time. For me, my family, our friends, and those officers, too. Forever seeing an empty red chair will signify one of the deepest pains that I could feel. A helpless feeling that burns deep inside, a pain that is tolerated over time yet never truly goes away. Many have felt that and know that pain; for others, it will come one day. It was real, it hurt, and it is part of life. It was awful. It still is awful. My very own chest hurts, with a strong ache; how could it happen just three hours apart? One life, one love, my parents were gone. Mom at about 7:15 p.m. and Dad around 10:15 p.m. on that cold Wisconsin night in February. Both of my parents were dead.

In the days following their deaths, I attempted to make sense of why my dad's chair was empty too. I did not go into their house for at least two weeks. I couldn't bear being there and replaying the night I found my dad over and over again in my head. What should I have done? Could I have saved him? How did this happen? So many questions and so much guilt inside me. Why didn't I save him? Why did I not get there sooner?

I wanted to feel his warm hug and hear his big belly laugh and growly voice. I yearned to hear his opinion on everything and everyone and listen to him tell one of his goofy jokes and make an odd noise that would accompany his weird, goofy self. His beard-covered face and his annoying comments. I missed everything about him. I missed my mom, too. Life was different now. I have family and people who love me and always have, yet in those days following my parents' deaths, I felt so alone. Maybe it's the unconditional love you miss—well, I know it is—yet the feeling of being alone can be hard to shake. Everything stands still for a time.

I do not think you can prepare to lose your parents. Though with my mom I managed to accept that she had cancer and that she would die, I was never ready, yet somehow she helped me understand that I would be okay. If you have or had a great mom, you know how they can do that. She made peace with her illness and helped me think about her quality of life and understand that she was not living when she was being defined by the hell of cancer. Remember, she had lived to die, and she made sure we were ready for her to die, too.

Dad, though, was gone with no notice, no chance to say goodbye. Mom was expected to die because of the cancer, but he was not. We were supposed to plan her funeral together; I was supposed to help comfort him, and he was supposed to help comfort me. Along with my sisters and family, we were supposed to get through my mom's death together. Now we found ourselves grieving both parents, our kids lost both grandparents and were grieving, and all the other friends and family, anyone that knew them, was grieving. The grief was double and it was deep.

Now that my dad was suddenly gone too, how were we supposed to know what to do next? It seemed so unfair. My mind was trying to understand how this had happened. How could my father pass away so soon after my mom? Yet it was the reality of life, and it can happen.

Somehow you find a way to push through the pain, or at least that is what I told myself. You have to turn off the switch, stop focusing on what happened, and start remembering the positive memories and focus on the good things around you in your life.

There was so much sadness in my life already, but I started to think about what had happened and remembered a message a friend sent me the day after my parents' deaths. It was simple and said this:

I know it feels like you are going through a tragedy right now, and you are in complete shock, but for some of us on the outside like me, you have to look at the blessing that it is. I know you are hurting, but to be able to leave this world on the very same day as your soulmate, what a wonderful gift that is for them. They get to continue their journey together forever, and that is something special.

Of course, I couldn't think about that in the weeks following, but eventually I did. There became a common theme at my parents' funeral—One Life, One Love—and somehow that started to stick, and the more I thought about it, the more I knew my dad would have been a miserable, grumpy mess without my mom. As much as I loved him, he certainly was a unique man who did not need a big social life and depended on my mom for his happiness. This man could not love another woman more, yet sometimes he loved her so much that his life would have been a disaster without her. This is a sad story to share, yet it helps to understand how much my dad would struggle to continue on in this life without my mom.

(Photo: My parents, Marge and Steve Minsky, in 1993. They enjoyed having fun together, and what I learned early on in life is how much my father leaned on my mother and how much she was his social life. He deeply loved his wife and I know he felt as though she saved him from the dysfunctional life he'd had leading up to their marriage.)

It's amazing that something as simple as Elvis' birthday can remind me how much I miss my parents. My dad's love for oldies music and Elvis certainly is something that has stuck with me. The song "Always on My Mind" seems to be the perfect song, first because they are always on my mind, and second, because it is the perfect song for my dad and mom and a great way to describe how much he loved her. Two days before they passed I was driving home with my dad from the hospital, and, being with my mom and clearly understanding that the end of her life was approaching faster than any of us were ready for, I turned on some oldies on the radio. My dad turned it off and said he couldn't listen. "Always on My Mind" was on.

With tears in his eyes, he said, "I can't do it, kid. I can't listen to the music and this song because I will never be able to dance with your mom again. I should have been a better husband, but she has to know how much I loved her."

He didn't say anything else on the way home. It was silent, he was silent, and it was sad. I fought back tears behind my sunglasses because I felt his pain. I know she prepared us, yet when you have a mom like mine, you are never ready.

Looking back on that moment, that memory, I have come to realize that my friend was right. My dad passed the same day and it had to be that way. He lived to die, and it had to be with my mom. That's eternal love.

Today, I believe they are dancing to Elvis and he is right where he needs to be, with Mom. True love was their reality; it was not always perfect but it was their one life, their one love, and my mom was certainly always on his mind and was the one he could not live without. If she was gone, naturally it made sense for him to go too. In the days after, as I dried my own tears, and still now, I am so comforted and grateful for understanding how strong his love for my mom was, because it has helped me heal. Now, when I hear his favorite music, it makes my heart swell and puts a smile on my face because it reminds me that love is why it hurts. It also reminds me that they are together and that is just the way it had to be. All of this has made me realize that I needed to stop thinking about why this happened and just let it be. I needed to stop thinking and start doing. Death is real, and when it happens, we hold on to it because to do so is easy. It is easy to get lost in the pain and use it as a cushion to hide from the world.

The reality is, that was not a way of life for me, for my husband, for my children, or for everyone else around me. I could not hide from the world, yet I used my parents' death to do just that. Although I didn't know how to start again or what to do, I had to do something. I could not allow myself to die inside, too.

My dad would have not been able to live through the grief of my mom's passing. I believe that. I believe he would have slowly died inside each day without her, and I also believe that I didn't need to let that happen to me. I needed to live again, find my passion again, and discover a way to push through the challenges if I ever wanted to find happiness and success again. We live to die and until we see the beauty of it, survivors of any kind of grief can die too. I didn't want to die and I hope you don't either.

Nearly Ninety Days
Written 90 days after their deaths
By Krista Sobieski

Nearly ninety days shouldn't seem so long,
Though the reality is that in our hearts we feel that you're gone.
Nearly ninety days our hearts skip a beat,
Though we know heaven is a front seat.
Nearly ninety days, forever time stops,
Though we try to make the feelings drop.
Nearly ninety days, we have to give it time,
Though it's hard, we let the clock chime.
Nearly ninety days, it hurts more each day,
Though it's hard, a deep pain will stay.
Nearly ninety days, two good-byes too soon,
Though we wonder if heaven's near the moon.
Nearly ninety days, it's okay to still cry,
Though we move on, our eyes will never dry.
Nearly ninety days, earth life moments apart,
Though time stands still, it's your new start.
Nearly ninety days, memories don't fade away.
Though we can't now, we'll see you another day.
Nearly ninety days, miss you Mom and Dad,
Though seeking peace, hearts remain so sad.

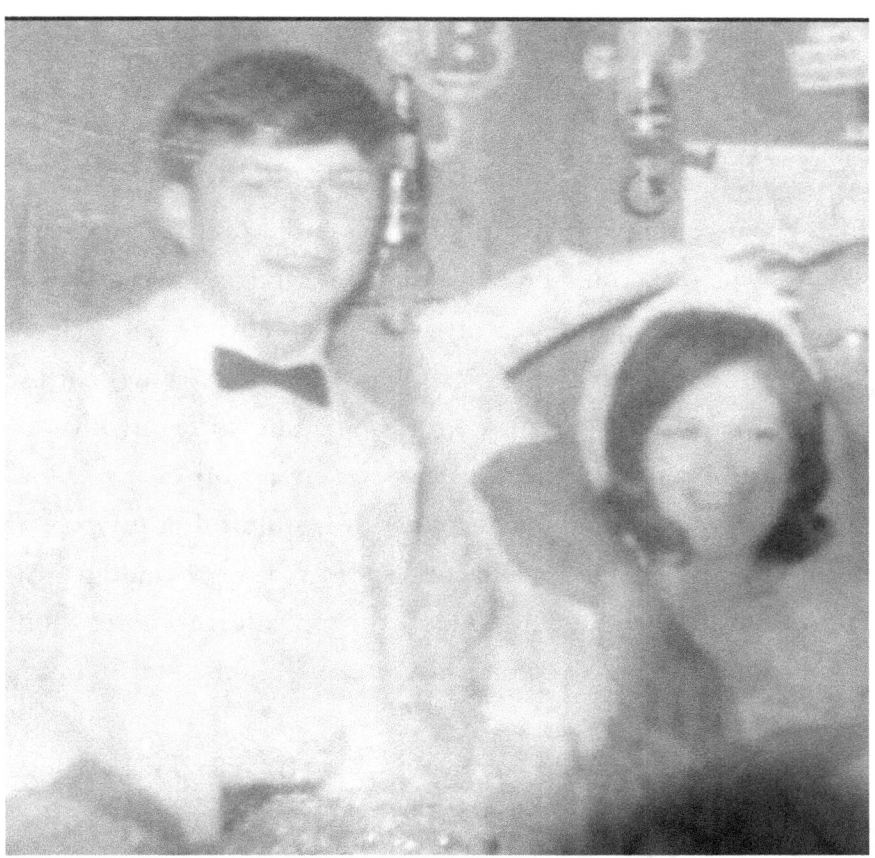

(Photo: Steve & Marge Minsky, Krista parents, were married on July 19, 1969 in Wisconsin. They shared 47 years of marriage together before passing away.)

The Nightmare Before

Prior to losing my parents, there was a nightmare happening in my world that I could have never predicted. One that would literally cripple me and, at the time, make me wonder if life could get any worse. You already know that I lost both my parents in a day, so you and I both know that life can always get worse, and it went from bad to worse quickly.

I was on top of my world, felt semi-successful in my career, and had already incorporated myself so I could fulfill my goal of becoming a professional trainer and speaker, as I was finding great enjoyment in helping all kinds of people learn more about leadership, teamwork, community collaborations, and building strong partnerships.

(Photo: This was me, Krista, in my work office in 2015, at the top of a career in early childhood. I worked with children and families for 23 years before starting to write and become an author.)

I began my career in early childhood education, which took me from being a preschool teacher to an administrator and business owner. I was involved in many things and organizations, and felt like I had made a difference in the world of early childhood education, where I'd started. I felt very well-respected in the industry and liked to think that people understood my dedication and passion and knew that I always tried to do my best when it came to work. I gave my career everything I had. Though I had four children, in some sense, my career was part of me and like another child. I loved my job and most of the people I worked with. I had dedicated and dependable people around me and I will never forget that. Despite many changes, I would still credit them with helping me do much of the work that I did. They were really great employees and, at the time, they were friends who were close to my heart. My only regret now is that no matter what, I was still the boss, and in the end, perhaps they saw me more as a boss than as a friend. That can be hard to understand in business when you really care about people. No matter what you do and no matter the decisions you make, many will often fault you rather than try to understand how hard the struggle is.

Anyway, things were going well, yet having a higher calling to do more, I started an action plan to transition the small private business I owned into a nonprofit. I knew it would be better for the children and families we served and for the community, too. I believed with all my heart that I personally was holding the program back, not able to give it the boost it needed, so I thought that giving it to the community would be the best option to help it grow. I had given what I could but it was time to look beyond, because as much as I had loved it, my passion was starting to change. The days were getting longer and I was in burnout mode, yet holding out hope that something good would happen.

Through a lengthy process and the support of the right people, eventually, the program became a nonprofit; now I wasn't the owner and it was governed by a board of directors. The original board was amazing, supportive, and committed to helping the program grow. They believed in the idea of it being a nonprofit and it was a beautiful collaboration that I felt really proud of. I could step away and focus more on the future. Things were looking brighter and I could not have been more delighted. I had wanted to take steps to focus on doing other things in my career and now was the perfect opportunity.

I was never prepared for what would happen in the spring of 2016, the nightmare before the deaths. I was now employed by the nonprofit and still helping to mentor the staff and the new people coming in to run the program. Things seemed positive and I knew that in time I would start to grow away from the program. Naturally, as I was no longer the owner, things would change. I expected that, I really did, and I was okay with it, yet somehow I always thought it would be a place where I would be welcomed back and that there might be some appreciation for the employees and myself for the work we originally did to build a respected business that people could trust. I had a lot of trust in the board members and I had a lot of trust in the new people in administrative roles, and for the most part, many of them were pretty good. I was blind not to see how destructive a few of them really were. My biggest regret is that I didn't see through the crudeness until it was too late. I have a soft spot and tend to believe the best of people, but slowly it felt like everything around me was crumbling.

You hire professionals to help and you trust that people are doing things for the greater good, but sometimes all it takes is one or two bad apples to make the whole bag rot. This is exactly what started to happen to me. There were a few bad apples around me that started to turn things sour fast. They were either that selfish, that unaware, or truly thought I was evil and were out to get me.

In the spring of 2016, prior to my parents' passing, I learned that a trusted accountant had not been filing the appropriate reports for the nonprofit, and, worse yet, led everyone to believe the work was done. I had worked in business long enough to know many things, yet was not experienced with nonprofit businesses, and trusted that he was doing what was right. Well, the center learned that he wasn't, and the state Department of Revenue and the Internal Revenue Service were breathing down everyone's necks and it felt like mine was being crushed.

Although I was on many of the business accounts, at this point in my career I did not handle the finances like I had when it was my own business. The biggest downfall was that none of us were really experienced, yet we trusted the accountant a lot. That is what you do when you expect professional services. No one should have, though. The hard news for me was yet to come.

Due to the accountant's negligence, a lot of things went wrong. I don't blame anyone, as I should have seen through it, although I honestly believed that between what the accountant was doing and the board reviews, business was going as usual. I just trusted in the process and everyone around me. I trusted faithfully. What I didn't expect was for the accountant and a couple of the bad apples on the board to turn their backs on me and attempt to throw me under the bus for no real reason other than the fact that they really wanted me out. Now, with the issues with the accountant, they wanted me to be responsible for the debt owed. We had two additional administrative people in the office, both of whom did a good job, although due to being inexperienced, they didn't see through it either, so in the end, it was easiest for some members of the board to blame me.

It was one of the worst times of my life. To go from being a respected business professional to being portrayed as a liar and having rumors spread about me was about the most hurtful thing a few individuals could ever do. There were two in particular who were sneaky, disrespectful, and self-centered, and to this day, though in my heart I have forgiven them, I am disappointed in them. I didn't think I could ever forgive them for not supporting me through this issue. Honestly, it's harsh, but they were downright self-centered individuals, and in my mind, they were never there for the greater good of the program, but for their own personal needs and those of their children. To this day, I am not sure I could ever look at either one of them without saying some choice words, yet I know in time they will face the redeemer, so that will be punishment enough. I can't change what they did or didn't do or how they made me feel; I just learned to tighten my circle, and I remain confident that somehow this matter has made me a better person.

They took what was a center dilemma and turned it into my problem. Most of the members either turned their backs on me or just walked away. The program director, who had full rein to grow her career, turned her back too. While she did not create the issues, she also could have helped resolve the issues, yet she turned her back on the program and on me as well. Naturally, I imagine she was scared, though when she stopped talking to me, I realized that, like the others, she was a bit self-centered as well. I didn't see through it early on, yet her final temper tantrum due to not getting her way in another matter was a great way for her to exit. I just never expected her to stop talking to me and turn several of the other staff against me. Her plan worked, even if she wasn't really trying, and while I never wish her bad luck, I am glad that I have not seen her since. It's a good thing, as I don't think I could stomach her fake goodness. She had her own personal agenda, too, and I don't think I would ever want to talk to her or see her again.

I gave her as much as I could, and what I learned later is that she was not really well-liked at all, and since then, things have not been easy for her, either. No wonder the original staff used caution and seemed distant. As time has passed, I certainly see why now. If only I had been smarter, yet, at the time, I thought she was helping. I thought she seemed like the right person to lead, so I could pursue other avenues and dreams. In the end, she turned out to be one of my biggest regrets, along with the bad board members who should have made a difference in the entire matter. They all walked away, making me out to be the one who should be responsible for the issues, and leaving everyone hanging. As a unit together, I believe that the problems could have been resolved and it would not have gotten to the game of pointing fingers. In my mind, I know the accountant is the one at fault, I will believe that always. What he did caused a lot of hurt, anger and sadness.

As stated, the nightmare began before my parents passed, and due to all the issues after they passed, the state and feds wanted their money owed by the center. Since I looked like the easy target to blame, that's what happened. I was on my own and I was told by those trying to help me to make an exit from the program right away. To protect myself, I had to file appeals with both the state and the Internal Revenue Service. An IRS agent, along with the lawyers, actually told me to leave the center right away and to stay as quiet as possible. When my parents were alive, I had not realized how awful this situation was, or perhaps I did not want to believe that it was that bad. I just trusted that it would work out; I didn't expect them to come after me. I had no idea that things would go from awful to terrible and didn't expect the mounds and mounds of emotions I would feel.

Though the state instantly found me innocent and the local IRS agent also found me not at fault, it doesn't always matter because someone wanted to get paid and they thought that I could pay. I was the new target, and those who had the power to change it didn't.

Since I owned the business before it became a nonprofit, it was natural for me to be a target and for me to be held responsible. When there is a situation that goes wrong, there has to be someone to blame and hold accountable and in this matter, that person was me. Having to hire an attorney and not be able to converse fully with my husband about the issue made me feel like I was being deceptive and unfaithful, because when you are in a marriage, you are to be honest, and I knew that in this matter, I had to protect him and my kids. Thank goodness for good attorneys and some of my parents' inheritance. Not only did someone want me to pay for the accountant's errors and the center's past-due payments, but within days of my parents' deaths, the board members were scratching around trying to look into my personal finances and even went as far as trying to have me investigated by the local police department.

At this point, I was not only trying to grieve my parents' deaths; I was attempting to grieve for the career I had once loved while remaining silent and discussing the matter with no one. I was told that to help myself, I had to keep quiet. Anyone who really knows me knows it was hard; I was so scared that I started questioning my own mind. Over and over again I questioned myself. I put myself down and lost a lot of confidence. I allowed others to get in my head and blamed myself for everything that life was throwing at me. The truth is, the IRS does really only send letters, and now, unfortunately, I know that. The worst part was when the board of directors had all of the IRS letters from the center sent to me by certified mail, along with a letter telling me that this was my fault and they expected me to resolve it. It is very interesting how everyone loves you until something goes wrong. It was a matter that could have been resolved as it was a central situation involving the entire organization, and the board and involved staff should have been standing together against the accountant who did not do his job. What I do know now, though, is that when people become scared or unsure of what to do, most will walk away in fear, and that's what happened.

One special person, who was like a dear mother to me, knew. She was a former school teacher who I reconnected with and was an original board member in the transition of the organization.

My previous board came to my rescue, as did a couple of the staff. They all wrote letters of no wrongdoing, and although they did not have a lot of detail and maybe did not understand the enormous challenge I was going through, I will always consider them my real-life, true angels and friends. They deeply cared about me and wanted to help me. It takes a person of courage to do what is right, and they were trying to help me.

My heart hurt. All of me hurt. My life was about as close to hell as it could get and I no longer had my mom to talk to. I was devastated. Everything in my life was turned upside down. My husband couldn't be told the whole story, because if he knew and was ever questioned, I was told that he could be found to be at fault, too. He worked damn hard for everything we had. I was sick. Really sick in my heart and my mind, and going crazy. Suicide was never an option, though. I am glad for that. I loved my family too much. I hated being put in this position, so I told myself I would remain silent. I wouldn't talk about it, I would not trash those who hurt me and turned their backs on me, and I would turn to my faith to find a way through this deep, dark tunnel. I felt deceitful to my husband and through it all, that was the hardest. I hated it.

A great attorney helped me prove my innocence to the state, though as I said, the IRS was a different story. They called in the big guns: a big tax attorney to help me. He believed in me, I think, and I had hope in him. Nearly four years and there were still no answers. I still was not relieved. Still my silence. Still my secret nightmare. When this was over, how would I ever tell my husband of this burden? He would be so disappointed, yet we had a strong love and commitment and I believed that he would find a way in his heart to forgive me. I only stayed silent to protect him and to protect our family from having to foot the organization's big bill.

(Photo: This is me with my husband in July of 2017, the year my parents passed away. Seeking refuge and hope, not being able to fully share my business story with him, to protect him and my family, beyond my parents deaths, it was one of the hardest times in my life.)

Life changed; I lost my motivation to speak, and I could hardly write anymore. All my desire for my new side business was put on hold. I started writing for a small newspaper, and enjoyed writing feature articles, but had a hard time with the hard news. They kept me, though, so I must have done something right. I still waited for a determination from the IRS with no end in sight. Once, the attorney and I thought it was coming in July of 2019, but still, they passed that date and had to look further and wait longer.

Slowly, I moved on with life, accepting that my parents were gone, and focused on my family. My husband, my kids. I kept myself busy writing for the newspaper and praying that somehow this nightmare would end. I read bible verses that were sent to me daily online, trying to focus on what each verse meant in my life at that moment. I watched for clues that life would get better. Slowly it did, and though I was waiting and waiting for an answer, I started to move on, yet deep in my heart I had this silent secret that was still ripping me apart. Would it ever end? Life moved on and I tried to, too, and I never gave up leaning on the hope that this would eventually pass. It was exhausting and holding me hostage. I could not let it go. It ate at me daily and an answer never seemed like it would come. Hope was all I was holding on to.

The Light That Comes

With everything that was going on, I needed to get my mind off of the negative things and focus on something positive, so I had this idea that maybe I should find a way to honor my parents. I tried planting flowers, I tried planting a tree. The tree died before I ever put it in the ground. I tried to go to the cemetery often to reconnect with my parents in a new way. I was hurting inside and needed to move forward. I was lost and, at first, did not know how to move on. Some days are still a struggle, yet I know they would want me to be happy. I know that. These days I struggle more with second-guessing myself than anything, yet like most struggles, as time passes, it gets easier.

I thought a lot about the conversations I'd had with my mom when she was dealing with cancer, and about how she told me to keep doing good in the world. I thought that maybe there was something bigger I could do. I love to do things for and give things to other people and I knew how great it felt. I needed to get back to that. So I thought that I could organize an event that would both honor my parents and do some more good.

When my mom was very ill, I made a promise to her that I would remain strong. She knew about the matter with the center and upon coming to the realization and acceptance that she most likely was going to die from the cancer, it became very hard to visit her without feeling hopeless. I still believe that she did seek treatment to try to beat her battle with cancer, yet I think she knew early on that it was going to be an uphill battle. During one particular visit I had with her, she was very sick and I started to cry. She told me that I needed to wipe away my tears and go home. She told me that my spirit was too big to be so sad and that I was stronger than I thought. It is ironic looking back on all our conversations. I realize now that during that time, I was trying to find ways to prepare myself for not having my mom physically here and she was holding on to prepare me and others for how to live life without her.

My mom and I did not always see eye to eye, and though I know in many ways we were very different people, we had a very close bond and she was my go-to person. She was sharing words of wisdom and told me that I was my best self when I helped others, so naturally, doing something that helped others was what I had to do. I had to follow my mom's advice and I knew that in order to get out of the black hole I felt like I was in and to find happiness in my heart, I needed to move forward, and helping others is how I would start to heal my own heart.

I had once thrown a '50s/'60s Rockin' Oldies Party as a fundraiser for the center, and it was well-received but never really took off. Maybe it wasn't personal enough to the center and more personal to me because I grew up on that kind of music. The music connected (and still connects) me to my parents and my childhood. It takes me back to simpler times, when life seemed more carefree and not full of worries. Music, I believe, was my father's outlet for the struggles he dealt with in life, and now it has become one of mine, too.

So, I talked to my husband and kids first. They were

concerned about me taking on more work, though they were supportive and kind about my desire to do it. I then reached out to someone who had been helping me with my parents' financial affairs and estate, as I knew he had knowledge of how to organize charities; I shared my idea and asked what he thought. I knew I wanted to do an event, yet, I knew that to be a true charity we needed to have nonprofit status. I knew that given what had happened at the last place I worked, I would never again employ people or go down the path of business ownership in the sense of working for a nonprofit, I just wanted to do good. He liked my ideas and from there I reached out to others.

(Photo: A Rockin' Oldies Dance Party is held annually, each spring in Berlin, Wisconsin to help raise funds to support the non-profit that was found in memory of Marge & Steve Minsky)

Eventually, the dance party to raise money was planned, and before we knew it, in the spring of 2018, Unimaginable Hope was organized. We were a new nonprofit with a mission to do good, spread kindness, and make a difference. With the support of so many wonderful people, this new light in my life gave me the hope I so desperately needed. I could have never realized how much this new charitable nonprofit, Unimaginable Hope, would impact my healing. We had planned the event with the hope that our nonprofit status certificate would be granted, and just a couple weeks before the first event, the letter from the IRS arrived in my mailbox, but this time it was the letter of designation, making me realize that even though others had hurt me and I still had a fight in front of me, I could find a new way to help others and continue to make a positive impact in the community and in our world.

This letter from the IRS was one I was honored to receive. People often are confused about how we made it all happen so quickly, and really, looking back, I have no idea how we did it. We put the cart before the horse, as some might say, and started planning the event before we even knew if we would be able to be a nonprofit. I like to think that my parents, my angels, were looking out for those of us trying to make this happen and that somehow, perhaps my mom had a hand in making it happen. She knew I needed the help and the support. The nonprofit was set up to help others, yet what I need others to understand is how much it helped me.

People were supportive and we started to raise money and collect donations. We help individuals who need help, we donate to groups and schools, and we started a program to help cancer and heart patients as well as a program to help teenagers obtain quality shoes when the need arises. Sometimes we help during tragic and tough situations, and other times we help because we want to be a positive force in the community and surrounding area. At my parents' funeral, we learned so much from those who shared stories about how they helped others, and this was a way we could continue to do that. The small things they did to help others made big impacts, and I wanted to carry that on. I wanted that to be their legacy.

(Photo: With my husband and children at the 2019 Rockin' Oldies Party. Learning to serve together and carry on the legacy of my parents' ability to impact others, has been a blessing in my life that has helped me heal.)

I soon learned how rewarding and healing it was to help others. I think that naturally I have always been a helper and have always had a desire to do positive things. Through Unimaginable Hope, I was finding that fire and fight that I lost when my parents passed and I was forced out of a career that I was once passionate about. In my heart, I know I was depressed, and though I did seek counseling once, the woman I went to, insurance dictated, talked to me more about how she helped those who had a gambling addiction. I didn't have a gambling addiction, I was grieving the loss of my parents, the loss of my career as I knew it, the loss of colleagues who were once my friends, and living a silent nightmare that I couldn't talk about out loud. This counselor was not helping me and I was embarrassed to ask others for help. It's sad, but my heart felt so much guilt, so much hurt, and I was so lost. I felt my life was shattered and the one person who was supposed to help me, the counselor, didn't.

So independent, for me, reaching out for help was hard, and I told nobody that I went for counseling. Nobody. The reality is, I had every reason to go to counseling, yet it made me feel defective and ashamed that I couldn't get through this on my own. Now I realize that what I went through was trauma. I didn't know that then. I lost so much and blamed myself. To me, trauma was when people were physically hurt, like in an accident. I did not see myself as suffering trauma and being impacted by finding my father deceased and going through the terror of the business ordeal. I had not realized how those things had hurt me.

I didn't take Mom right away for a second opinion about her cancer. I did not see how sick my dad was with heart issues. I did not know that the accountant was not doing his job. I did not know the financial reports were wrong. I did not know how to fix everything and I felt like I had let so many people down. I let my parents die, I let the families and staff down at the center, and I had to be dishonest to my husband and kids. I didn't know that I needed counseling, and when I tried, the counselor I went to wanted to talk about gambling. I wasn't a gambler. I did not gamble with money, yet maybe I was taking a gamble on other things, and perhaps that is why all this bad stuff was happening. Maybe I was a different kind of gambler who took risks, trusted others, and loved with my whole heart. I wasn't a gambler, yet my heart hurt like I had lost millions.

My heart was hurting so badly, but somehow through Unimaginable Hope and the grace of God, I pushed through. Through this organization, I found a way to help others because it was the only thing helping my heart heal. It gave me hope; it gave me something to feel good about and something to look forward to. I know I was depressed and through it all, Unimaginable Hope, my loving husband and kids, and everyone who supported this idea filled my heart with new peace, a peace I so desperately needed.

Then, suddenly, in the spring of 2022, almost six years later, the incident with the IRS was resolved. I was found not liable for any of it. I was cleared and it was like a weight lifted. Yet, as good as it was, no one really knew it happened. Very few understood my tears of joy and there were very few people to celebrate with. It was sad. I was relieved, although not many knew the silent hell I had gone through over those six years. Unimaginable Hope was honestly what helped me through it all. The light had come. The tunnel of darkness was no longer lingering over my head. At least that was my hope. My dear friend who was like my mom was the only person I could really celebrate with, other than the attorney.

My friend sent me flowers and it did make it better, even though my broken heart still felt like I had deceived so many people by not being able to share my story.

Finally, I can share my side. Thank goodness, I am here to let others know that I never did anything bad, I just trusted the wrong people. That is what is interesting about life. Not everyone is mean and untrustworthy, yet all of this robbed me of some real happiness. My confidence had been taken, I felt forced to walk away from a career I once loved, even though I wanted a new challenge at that time and most likely would have left the center, I never expected to have to say goodbye to a business I was so honored to be a part of. Watching it grow and having to leave it without being able to share why, was very sad. It was great to *win* in this matter, and to know that I was not being held responsible for someone else's mistakes was rewarding, yet healing from having to walk away was still an internal battle for me. In my mind, I felt worthless, and in my mind I continued to question how this all happened. The deaths made me feel more alone, as I was unable to tell my parents. Finally I had been cleared, yet as a Christian, I suppose I should believe that they know, and perhaps even had a hand in helping me.

Love, Life, and Relationships

N ow, as life continues, I feel compelled to share what I have felt and learned. It's just my thoughts, and my hope is that somehow this story, the words that I have shared, will help someone else; it will help others in the face of darkness to give in to hope.

(Photo: My husband and kids are the reason I was able to give into hope and thrive. My love for them pussed me to find a way through the challenges I faced and move on. It all hurt, yet love was greater.)

If you are fortunate, you will experience unconditional love. I did, and it was from my parents. Our life was not perfect, but I know that my parents did love my sisters and me unconditionally. They didn't give us everything we wanted, but they gave us what we needed and taught us to be independent. They raised us to take care of ourselves and taught us how to be good people, even if we are not perfect.

If you are lucky, you will have the right people around you

whom you can really trust, but always be cautious. If you have a kind heart, it can easily be hurt by those you least expect. Trusting others in a cruel world is hard. I thought I could trust people and believed that, like me, others had good intentions. What I learned is that people are more selfish than we think. It doesn't mean everyone is dishonest, it just means that you should follow your instinct on character. Might save you some hard days ahead. It will also save you from dealing with trust issues. I am still working on that. It's hard not to want to believe the best in people.

If you are sensitive like me, you will get taken advantage of, and even if your kind heart has the best intentions, it will be hurt by greed at some point. I have learned that people in this world can be cruel, and no matter how much you want to believe differently, some don't have the capacity to be good. Do not beat yourself up over it. Some people are sensitive. Just know that it is part of who you are; the reality is, sensitive people tend to be empathetic, too, and it is never a bad quality to understand the story of another person or situation.

On the flip side, there are also kind, loving people. Sometimes it's okay to keep the circle small. I love my family and a few close friends, but who do you go to with issues? Trust is hard when you feel like you are letting others down. Everyone has it in them to be kind, so what I have learned is that it is easier to be kind, and like me, you have no idea what a person is going through. The right people show up in your life at the right time. I didn't see it at the time but I did have a kind friend, a kind lawyer, and the right people who showed up when I needed them. I had kind people show up after my parents passed, too. Kindness costs absolutely nothing, so don't be afraid to spread it. It comes back tenfold. Yes, in time, it really does.

Life is only as hard as we make it. I made my life hard for nearly six years. I was stuck in grief and I lost my self-confidence. It happens. It happens more easily than you think, yet it's important to find a way out. It's okay to ask for help. I did try so many times to ask for help, and when I finally went to counseling, I was turned off by someone who I think did not know how to help me. Don't give up on finding the right people to help you. There should not be shame in seeking professional help. There is a reason people train to do their job, and there is a reason you should seek help. Maybe you don't need to seek professional help, yet know that if you are feeling like you might, don't hesitate—it will save you a lot of misery. Don't wait. Don't wait six years like I did. It's not worth your mental health. Independence is a great attribute to have, but there are some things we don't need to go through alone, so don't. Ask for help.

Communicate with those you love. The last moment can happen at any time. Time and time again, we never say the last words we want to. I am so grateful that I took the time to help my mom when she was battling cancer. I am so grateful for every moment I had with my dad, too, though it never seems like enough. If I could go back and have one last hug, one more chance to say "I love you," or one more time to just tell them that I did appreciate the childhood they provided my sisters and me, I would be so delighted.

Death is real. It will happen. We live to die. Yes, that's right, we live to die and we all will one day. Most of us won't plan the exact day or time, so love every freaking moment that you can. Love. Love. Love. Love hard. It hurts to have lost so much, yet it's because of the love. I loved my parents and they loved me back. I loved my original career, and it hurt to feel forced out. Love makes everything hurt harder, yet in the end, know that it is so worth it. Love also helps you on hard days. One day your smile will return just as mine did, and you will think of the memories and find a way to laugh again. Believe that the best is yet to come. Sometimes during hardships, the only thing we can hold on to is the idea that things will turn around. Hold on to that thought. Stay optimistic and know that it will get better. It may seem like forever, but with a focused mind, it will get better. Always give into hope. Always.

(Photo: Death is so real. You can't imagine it until you experience it, yet we can not change it. The loss of my parents changed my life, yet what they taught me early in life is that you must move on and keep moving forward.)

A little bit more on suffering a great loss. We have to remember that navigating grief is a deeply personal and challenging journey. It is very important to allow yourself to feel. That was one of the single biggest challenges that I had. Grief is overwhelming; it's easy and natural to avoid painful feelings and emotions. It is important to allow yourself to feel sadness, anger, frustration, and other emotions, as it is essential for healing. When we hide our emotions, it prolongs the grieving process and has an impact on our whole well-being, from health to healing. Always understand that feeling pain is normal and you have to go through it to heal.

As I stated earlier, you have to seek support and find ways to stay connected. For me, even Unimaginable Hope was my support group in some ways. It allowed me a place and platform to share what had happened to my parents and allowed me to share my story. It provided me with a place to share my experience with loss and hear others' stories. Connecting with others in this way can be very comforting, and you don't always have to feel so alone. It's hard to understand how we process grief and how others around us process it differently. It can take each person a different amount of time and space to get through grief. For some, prayer and faith can provide hope during a time of loss, yet even for the faithful it can be hard to understand how loss can happen. It's normal to question faith and not truly have instant peace or understanding of why loss happens. It takes time and grace to feel fully content and at peace.

It hurts to lose people. In my case, I felt a strong love that made the loss seem unbearable, yet for others it might be entirely different. Experiencing death may leave a deeper emotion as there may have been a disconnect or loss of relationship, unspoken words of love, and gratefulness. We never get time back. One thing I do feel is some peace in knowing that I was able to help my parents and be there when my mom was sick. It was not always easy and there were times when I felt uncertain and frustrated with not being able to just have a normal schedule, yet now I feel thankful for all the extra time I had with them. Even more so after losing my dad. I would have never had the extra conversations driving to appointments and being with them. It altered my schedule a lot. I know there were times my frustration was over the top and yes, I did get angry at times, yet it was my choice to be there. I wanted to be and I could be, so I did. I know there were others in my family and friends around us who would help, yet now I am so thankful that I was there. Time is one thing that is not known, and even though we think we have all the time in the world, at any moment our lives can change and we can lose people we love.

I think that my entire story shares how quickly things can change and how much we need to be reminded that we can not take anything or anyone for granted. One moment I was on top of my career, raising my kids with my husband, enjoying life, when everything started to crumble. During the crumbling, truly giving in to hope was the one thing that I could do. If I am being honest, journaling and writing also helped save me. It gave me a way to express my feelings so I didn't feel like I was burdening others. For some it might be creating art or another hobby that helps fill the void of losing those you love, feeling forced to change careers, or facing unexpected situations that bring you down. It's important to remember to find healthy ways to express your feelings and verbalize and take control of your emotions. We can not release how we are feeling if we can not process our emotions.

Taking care of physical health is also important, and grief and change can take a big toll on our bodies. It's hard to sleep when we experience trauma, and yes, as a reminder, grief is trauma. When we experience or go through difficult situations it alters how we think, how we respond, and how we move forward. Exercise and eating are healthy habits that lift our energy and that we must prioritize as part of our healing, too. Many people do not fully understand that our physical well-being is connected to emotional healing and it really is vital that we take care of ourselves.

(Photo: Being able to honor my parents and share their story through Unimaginable Hope has been a joy for me to do. I can never physically bring them back, yet their memory remains constant through the services we do in their name.)

Honoring our loved ones is as important as honoring our feelings. I don't think I would have ever planned to create a nonprofit and would not expect it to be something everyone would or could do. My story of losing my parents on the same day was unique to me and seemed unbelievable at the time. However, as more time passes and as I connect with more people, the stories of others and learning about how they have been challenged has also helped me cope. You do not have to form a nonprofit or host a big event, yet you must honor what is hurting you. If it is the loss of a loved one, create a memorial, plant a tree, or engage in an activity that honors the person you've lost, and remember to honor yourself. Maybe you are not grieving a loved one but going through a tough situation. Honor the situation and really dig deep to process it. Release the emotions and move through it so that you can begin to heal.

Finally, remember that grief is a natural process, and there is no right or wrong way to navigate it. Be gentle and kind with yourself, seek connection, allow healing to unfold at its own pace, and seriously, understand that there will be times in life when you feel so alone. You will feel like there is no one to turn to. Experiencing death can make us feel alone, and going through bad situations can make us question our own sanity, affect our decisions, and make us uncertain of the right direction to go, yet in time, and though some things may never make sense, the greatest gift you can give yourself is the blessing to be okay, and understand that it's okay to heal and feel life again. We all have the power to feel our purpose and when we allow ourselves to feel whole again; that is where the magic happens.

No Obstacles in The Way

Don't wait to wake up and come alive. On depressing days, you will want to stay in bed, hide away, and not be alert to the world. Stop now and don't deprive yourself of happiness. For me, through it all, I found that spending time with my husband and kids, attending events with them, going to dinner with them, and having them around, is part of what started to help heal my heart and the hurt. I hope that every single person who reads this book has someone or something that helps see them through. My husband works a lot, sometimes too much in my opinion, but like me, he does it out of a place of love. I know that. It was hard on the days he was not home much and for me, keeping busy with my kids' activities and events made a world of difference. I know that not everyone has children or a spouse to help them like mine did; I just hope you find someone. My family did not even know how much they were helping me. They didn't know as they did not know how bad things were for me, crushing on the inside. They were not aware of my feelings and how concerning the situations at hand had been for me. Most had no idea how bad the situation was with the center and how much liability the state and IRS were after me for. No clue. They could not understand, as they didn't know, so how could they help me? They most likely assumed my sadness was from the loss of my parents. It was a combination, yet I tried to wake up happy. Happy for them, every single day. I would do anything to protect them, anything to make sure they knew how much I love them.

(Photo: Sometimes nature speaks to us and I take refuge watching for the signs of internal life around me. Capturing images of the sunrise and sunsets is something that brings peace to my heart. The glimpse of a sunrise, with the sun piercing through the clouds reminds me that heaven is for real and that's where I believe my parents are.)

One day, like me, I hope that you wake up and realize that no matter what obstacle is in your way, you have the ability to make choices and make a difference in your own life and those of the people you love. You deserve to be happy. You may not feel like it, and your self-confidence may be gone. You may feel like you have failed yourself and those you love, yet know that you have not. Failure and hurdles make us stronger. We cannot always see that. There will be so many things that cloud our thinking. Yes, it will be hard to understand, but one must realize that all that clouded thinking is really called trauma. When we go through messy ordeals in life, it is a form of trauma, and trauma causes us to shut down, lose our spark, and put obstacle after obstacle to really living a truly fulfilled life in our way. Trauma does not allow us to live like we're dying or to enjoy life because it alters everything we do, and so often inside it feels like we already did die. It is hard to see beyond the struggles and believe that things are going to get better, yet with all my heart, I kept giving into hope, that someday, this would all be just a bad memory.

It took me six years to wake up. Six years of my life were almost wasted worrying about what I could not control. I could not control the death of my parents. I could control how I reacted and how I honored their legacy. That I made it through okay. Creating Unimaginable Hope was a blessing in disguise, and while it was helping others, it really was healing my heart. I could not control what happened at the center and even though it was hard, I did not crumble. I felt like I failed but the reality is, I took every ounce of confidence I had left and I fought. I fought the state and the IRS and the people who wanted to blame me and walk away. It took forever, but there was victory. Yes, it cost me money to fight, and yes, it was hard going through, but I won! I proved that I did nothing wrong. I made myself feel guilty for six years. I was ashamed that I trusted people who I believed in but in the end, I prevailed! Yes, I was not held accountable for the debt of another's errors, and it takes perseverance to not give up. I felt like I had, but now it's easier to see it differently. I sought redemption for my family, for my financial security, and for myself, and I did not fail. I did what I had to do to survive and take care of what went wrong, and though every single day was scary and hard, that awful financial situation was rectified in some way and it no longer involved me, so for that I was grateful.

I lost six years of my life not taking control of it. I wish I had not done that and I am learning to leave the past in the past now. I am using my gift of writing to share my story in hopes that it helps another person. I hope that, like me, others can find a way to move forward and see the light after the darkness. I have so many reasons to be happy. I have a great husband, I have four awesome kids, I have a beautiful home, and the ability to use my God-given mind to make a difference in my own life and the lives of others. I have so many blessings and even though I could not see them throughout those six years, I see them now. I have so much to share, and although at times I wonder if all of this matters, somehow, I know in my heart that it does. It matters to me, because writing and sharing this story makes me realize that I am human and we all go through hard times. Times that hurt us, that ground us, and that humble us, and I know that when I leave this world, I may have not made the most money, I may not have won the most awards, and I may easily be forgotten, yet I hope to think that along the way, I may just have provided that one ounce of hope that someone else needed to survive another day.

As I end this story, I hope that every person who reads it can relate to something in my words and I hope that it gives them the will to persevere through the toughest times and take every chance they can to be extremely happy. Life is just too darn short, and even though I no longer trust the words "It can't get any worse," I can now finally trust my own judgment and instinct to know that I do make a difference in this world, and so do you. Everyone has a story, and like mine, yours deserves to be told.

Every day we learn new things, and every day is a chance for growth. It's up to us what we want. Sometimes you have to take all of the negative and turn it into something positive, giving yourself a quick glimpse of unimaginable hope that lets you believe that the best is yet to come. I did that, and I am living proof that you can survive the most unlikely circumstances. I am proof that when you give into hope and you learn to live to die, life can be whatever you choose for it to be. We can not control or change what happens to us, good or bad, yet we can decide how to react and how to overcome unfortunate circumstances.

I still have a lot to learn, yet I know I will always give into hope and take my mom's advice to "live to die." Maybe one day, like my parents, I can leave a legacy, too, by making a positive impact in one person's life, and so can you. No matter what, we must live life in a way that fulfills us and in which our stories matter. Everyone's story matters. Always believe that. It took me a while to understand that, especially on the worthless, guilty-feeling kind of days, but now I understand how and why my story matters and how I can make a difference. I have finally learned that I have something to give, not something to prove, and the most beautiful opportunity that I have is to be myself and honor my own story, for me, for those who love me, and as a way to really live a free, fulfilling life. Rather than continuing to look at the setbacks and always see them as a struggle, I have learned to contend with all that has been dealt. It has helped me grow, rather than remain the victim in my own reality.

You, too, can contend with anything, and think of how powerful that will be. Life is meant to be lived and enjoyed, and it's up to each of us to make the best of it. We live in a world where we can tell the truth over and over again and explain it so many times, yet a lie can be believed blindly. Somehow, when we learn to stop second-guessing ourselves and honor the face of the truth, it's really very freeing. The reality is, in the end, we really are responsible for ourselves, how we interact, how we respond, and how we move forward, so do yourself a favor and live. Live in a way you deserve and make the best of the time you have. I am finally grateful that I am doing that and I know you can too.

(Photo: My parents and I on my wedding day in 1997. I am, because of them and I cherish the memories I shared with them. Time is the only gift we can't get back and I am grateful for the time I had in life with them.)

Another lesson that all of this has taught me is that my purpose is much bigger than my circumstances. We have to accept that we can't change what is happening around us, we can only really choose how we react and how we overcome it, and even though my story has robbed me of some great times, I have also realized that fear is what stops us, and when we start to embrace what we are unable to change, we can fully start to live more confidently, and we will survive and learn to really enjoy life. As individuals, we are the only ones standing in front of our own dreams and moving through our own darkness. When we learn to find the support we need, ask for help, and continue to believe in ourselves, we can move forward. I finally was able to, and now, I am looking forward to enjoying life, really enjoying life, and you can too.

Writing this book was perhaps another way for me to release, to share my story, and while at times I have questioned the worth of writing it, I have accepted that there may be some who read it and don't relate to it or question what is written, yet it's my truth and I have come to the consensus that if it helps one person and gives them hope or the courage they need to move forward, then writing this book was worth it. My purpose has been served and I have given someone the opportunity to connect to my story and relate in a way that helps them. Giving in to hope sometimes is the only gift we have and if it has saved me, perhaps it can save others who have a hurting heart. We all serve a purpose and we all deserve to live truly authentic lives and this book is my truth. I have been on the top, I have been worried and fearful, I have felt hopeless and shattered. I have grieved hard and I have loved hard and felt confused and ashamed, yet somehow, by giving in to hope and holding on to every last ounce of goodness I could find to share, it helped me. It helped heal the darkness in my life, and by doing good for others, and hearing their stories, the feeling of being alone started to diminish.

The reality is that we can not control what happens in our life. I could not change that my parents had passed, I could not change how people hurt me or how it felt, all I could do is look at the blessings in my life and keep my mind focused on helping others, so that I could help myself. My kids, my husband, my family, my friends, and viewing life as a gift are what kept me striving and hoping that all of the hurt and lessons would be behind me. Hope is what saved me and as long as you hold on to that, you can get through anything. Be authentic, be hopeful and have the courage to share your story; it will set you free.

Unimaginable Hope

Unimaginable Hope is a charitable corporation that grants random acts of kindness while meeting or fulfilling the needs of individuals, groups, and organizations. Spreading kindness and hope is a vital part of the work that Unimaginable Hope does. Unimaginable Hope will distribute funds and resources to assist, ensure and provide hope for those in need and for those working to make a difference in the world. The charitable work of the organization will be given in non-biased ways as funds allow it to meet the needs of many through the contributions it gives. Strictly charitable goals allow Unimaginable Hope to give in simply deserving ways. This organization is about instilling kindness through sharing and giving while attempting to make a difference in the world. To learn more about the organization please go to unimaginablehope.org.

(Photo: May the memory of my parents, Marge & Steve Minsky and the life and love they shared be remembered always.)

Thoughtful Seed Project

Planting an inspirational seed, the Thoughtful Seed Project is designed to help influence and encourage those following to a happier, more peaceful life. Learn to live more content in life every second of every day. Learn how to make a difference in everything you do by growing strong roots to create balance and security for a life filled with beauty, wonder and joy.

The Thoughtful Seed Project blog is geared towards helping readers live a happy, peaceful and confident life. The blog focuses on everyday topics that we live through in life. The idea behind the Thoughtful Seed Project is to be so busy loving life, you have no time for hate, regret or fear. As a freelance writer who enjoys helping her clients find the right wording for all of their personal and professional needs through the thoughtful seed project, Krista can assist in drafting and writing newsletters, website copy, creating flyers, managing social media posts. She can assist in helping update company profiles, writing articles and even help plan and organize your next event. Or if you need a ghostwriter to help you write your book. You can reach Krista Sobieski by email at kjsobie@gmail.com.

Looking to write a solo book or part of an anthology and need help with writing or publishing? Reach out to Krista Sobieski today, as an affiliate of She Rises Studio, she can connect you to the resources you need!

Would you like to order more copies of Giving into Hope or inquire about having Sobieski speak at your next event?
Email: kjsobie@gmail.com

To learn more about author Krista J. Sobieski, the Thoughtful Seed Project, the services offered or to learn more about Unimaginable Hope, the non-profit, the author founded please use the following links:

www.thoughtfulseedproject.com
www.unimaginablehope.org

About the Author

Krista Sobieski is the founder of the Thoughtful Seed Project of Central Wisconsin. A farmer's wife and mother of four who has a strong background in early education, leadership development, and community collaborations and loves to write and share her voice. She writes about topics including life, death, parenting, fundraising, motivation, and teamwork just to name a few. Krista lives in the country, believes in the greater God, and has worked in an early childhood setting for 23 years. She is the founder of Unimaginable Hope, a non-profit charity with a mission to spread kindness and bring hope to those who need it. In a moment of darkness, Unimaginable Hope was created when she lost her parents in three hours, on the same day.

LinkedIn: <u>linkedin.com/in/krista-sobieski-12608326</u>

Facebook: <u>www.facebook.com/kjsobieski</u>

Website:
<u>www.thoughtfulseedproject.com</u>
<u>www.unimaginablehope.org</u>

www.ingramcontent.com/pod-product-compliance
Lightning Source LLC
Chambersburg PA
CBHW070940120626
46546CB00004B/1488